CADAVER, SPEAK

Also by Marianne Boruch

MARIANNE BORUCH

Cadaver, Speak

Copper Canyon Press

Port Townsend, Washington

Copper Canyon Press is in residence at Fort Worden State Park in Port Townsend,
Washington, under the auspices of Centrum. Centrum is a gathering place for artists
and creative thinkers from around the world, students of all ages and backgrounds, and
audiences seeking extraordinary cultural enrichment.

LIBRARY OF CONGRESS CATALOGING-IN-PUBLICATION DATA

Boruch, Marianne, 1950–
[Poems. Selections]
Cadaver, speak / Marianne Boruch.
pages cm
ISBN 978-1-55659-465-6 (alk. paper)
I. Title.
PS3552.O75645C33 2014
811'.54—dc23

2013030001

3 5 7 9 8 6 4 2
FIRST PRINTING

COPPER CANYON PRESS
Post Office Box 271
Port Townsend, Washington 98368

www.coppercanyonpress.org

to Forrest, his first hundred years to come,

and for James Judkins, beloved irrepressible uncle-in-law

They undressed the corpse, but had no time to take
the gloves off; a corpse in gloves.

ANTON CHEKHOV

There is great Similarity between a Muscle and a Nerve.

JOHN KEATS

Having run out of paper,
I am writing on your rough draft.

ANNA AKHMATOVA

Contents

CADAVER, SPEAK

First

it's given. Then made.
Until the dying one says *Dream, undream me.*

Fragment to pattern, to inscription
in dust, on leaf, across any
cardboard box in the dumpster.

He climbs a ladder to scrape then paint
one side of the house each summer into fall.
Or he skips a few years. Another winter
ringed by a keyhole. And the door, what of

the hinge, little cry that won't uncry itself—

I

Face

On winter's long red-eye out of Anchorage, small lamps
near the floor made
a grainy blurry everything, which meant
awake, then almost, then heads slipping back
or to the side, mouths jarred open.
There are words
bodies vanish to—*curved, slumped, relaxed, released.*
And a sound, not the underwater lament of the whale, not its
distant me to you, don't even imagine.
I heard no sad rattle
from the human throat, only the loose tic-tick of it, seats 3A
to 10C, at last the whole cabin caught
in night's breathing, a dark sandpaper at work, stopped,
to start again.

The fact is I walked through an underworld, that aisle—
I was up, had to—and saw in the dim
not-yet-dawn the arms
and legs of Shiloh and Gettysburg flung
every which way.
Then past that easy horrific—
those strangers merely out, gone out,
curled to each other: love
in the abstract, love
how it never comes on purpose,
no one arranging a face to please or to frighten
into love, just a simple forgetting who
is who and if ever. Like children don't know the most
troubling thing about themselves, won't
for years. Or like the dead who could, but can't tell you.

For once I stared everyone right
in the face like it was
my shroud, and my leaving. I keep thinking *like.*

But my same nothing at all had so little
to do with it, that
one time my grandmother didn't say where
we walked, *took,*
I was taken, thrust forward to meet the old
blind woman, her hands to find
me in that child, the great length and breadth of her bent
as if to some odd-angled stone on a beach
so foreign, so much a place I'd never go, her barest
touch on my cheek coming
such a long way
to my chin and lips, the ridge of my nose, my
closed eyes. I opened them
to her face. Most private part of the body now, hugely
calm, the kind that suspends
and lets go, her eyes
blue in their milky drift regardless, looking
not anywhere or straight into, this—
no end to it, flying over a continent of
ice and sleep and ruin and light.

Pencil

My drawing teacher said: Look, think, make a mark.
Look, I told myself.
And waited to be marked.

Clouds are white but they darken
with rain. Even a child blurs them back
to little woollies on a hillside, little
bundles without legs. Look, my teacher
would surely tell me, they're nothing

like that. *Like* that: the lie. *Like* that: the poem.
She said: Respond to the heaviest part
of the figure first. Density is
form. That I keep hearing *destiny*

is not a mark of character. Like *pilgrimage*
once morphed to *mirage* in a noisy room, someone
so earnest at my ear. Then *marriage* slid.
Mir-aage, Mir-aage, I heard the famous poet let loose
awry into her microphone, triumphant.

The figure to be drawn—
not even half my age. She's completely
emptied her face for this job of standing still an hour.
Look. Okay. But the little

dream in there, inside the *think*
that comes next. A pencil in my hand, its secret life
is charcoal, the wood already burnt,
a sacrifice.

Old Paintings

Someone always lifted into heaven—
the Son, Mary, the Holy Ghost in perpetual
hover, any number
of saints alone. Or a *murder* of them,
those martyrs, their gorgeous flight north
reward for fire, for stones, hot breath in the ear.
Tooth and claw, human style,
down centuries like a drip.

Night trains now, one from Milano to Roma,
blue blanket, blue sheets in the sleeping car,
a sink, a shelf, all racketing, lurching
over mountain, vineyards, cutting goat trails in half.
Human nature. The ticket guy
won't warn us about it: someone keeps trying
our locked door all night. I hear that.
Then I dream that.

Violent too, how the paintings
rest, gallery after gallery
at the Vatican. Saint Sebastian, his arrows in deep,
up to their feathers. And the crucifixions—*this is the deadest
dead Christ we've seen,* my husband says, the skin
pasty gray unto green, the head lolling.
Then Saint Bartholomew (my grade school named for him,
I walked through his door), he can't unlove
being flayed, standard
pie plate of halo off-gassing golden behind him.
I thought that ended it, passing
into funny
because of distance. Could.

It didn't. Not the train,
not the door and door all night,
the rattle, dark
window of it nailed right to the wall.

Reason

The barber pole, the cheer
of red white   red white
turns out to be

the bloody bandage, a stump
in need of....

They weren't much good at it, the barber-surgeons
all over London, early 1800 whatever,
sooty air, barking dogs.

Factoid two: use of the murderer's body
in dissection labs then
(closed down in summer, given the stench).

Because everyone else's—not much
but mine own!—had to be
handy, intact for Heaven's last judgment,
most radiant there-on-out, body
you step *into* and
maybe it wants you back. Oh logic,
earning a bad name.

As for the murderer—good luck in hell, pal,
no one said too loud over
his various bits.

I guess most things have reason.
It subtracts, it multiplies.

Like when my steely handsome uncle delivered me home
after a long car ride, turning to my mother—
something's wrong with this child, she does not speak.

Forget windshield hypnosis, cornfield
after cornfield, forget
uncle/aunt silhouettes, front seat, pointing out
to each other
their pointing out anything.

My uncle beautiful, emphatic,
my mother nodding, too worried
to be convinced, not
laughing quite yet.

Future or past, it's all we ever think about.

At the Forum

Outside, one statue keeps its head.

And inside the museum, so many puzzle pieces missing
in the frescoes. Missing: a belly, a neck, an arm.

Among the upright stone figures, one
can't really bear it, another leans in
to the touch. Heads crooked, eyes closed—
pain or ecstasy, who can tell.
Sleepers dream like that, passing through tunnels
of rest, unrest.

The point is sweet or not sweet at all, a face
staring down or straight on.
Hair curls uncombed until a headband stops it.
So many noses
just not there. Skin *like* skin, ribs rough enough
shine under. The fragile scrotum, made of
stone now too, belies its grief
that the penis is gone. Shoulders draped
in the most opulent scarves fierced out, shattered,
soothed by mallet, by chisel. *Opulent.*
I never wrote
that word before. Others rise like

some moon-soaked cloud: *Subgrundaria,*
graves under the eaves. *Bidentalia,* places struck
by lightning—toxic, dangerous.
A rock buried there equals *bolt.* So that's settled.
Just in case, a fence went up around it.
More marking: *Pratica di Mare, Ficana,* and *Ardea*—the edge
they buried infants, children under ten,
to claim property, 620 BC. It works. The wind cries.

In the museum, it's over and over how those who walk and look
gaily ape the statues for the photograph home,
arm raised when
a stone arm is up, head turned
the same frozen angle.

To see and see. What to say. The bent figure of a woman
made of that stone.
A small hand on her lower back.
Nothing else left of the child once attached to it.

The Small Hours

for EDB

At Scrabble, challenged once, looking
down the page, my old cousin
goes wry over the next word: uranium—
"a useless element." *Time to
throw out the dictionary!*

Distinctly her voice. The past, you hear it
the small hours,
sucked down the undertow.
*Oh, that
sea of dream,* my cousin is saying.
She loved the cat
that nursed at her shirt. Evening all day,
the wet spot wide
as an island. They both fell asleep.

Sound by sound, death gets bigger
than dark. One is
a mouse in the wall and we hissed him
a scare. One is a door. One is a window in rain
we jammed with matchbooks
to quiet. One breathed my cousin
back as I dreamt.

Too many things
trouble night. *Dying's
just horseplay!* my old cousin singing
not impossibly glad. Bright strip
of room, a car,
a stop out there, a turn.

You've got to be kidding—that's
how to relish. Then she savored.
No afterlife about it! my old cousin
out of somewhere.

Skinny Fat

A skinny person once fat
is still prey to the fat that waits out
every run, every breathless
try again, or a bike
at the drugstore a moment, whoever it is
ducking inside for something not

really crucial. None of it's crucial
as this is crucial: keeping the bulky bloated
animal at a distance, albeit
an *albatross* distance but not like the guy
in Coleridge's opium-lovely rant who
couldn't, stopping to tell and tell and nearly
choke with his story that poor
wedding guest who just wanted to get to the party
and eat himself senseless.
Truth = the fable
of truth.

One sits in the body. One stands in it.
How peculiar. And some call that skinny thing
soul. But what if
the fat thing, that wanting,
is soul. And there's no final size to it, not even
a voice but when you sleep
a noise lightly or loudly rhythmic you
can't hear, a nothing
wired to a sea-bottom dark
or in the earth's deepest down
where I'm told

there is only a burning, as fat is said
to burn slowly, never
enough of it and never going out.

It Could Be

any school ends like
chalk dust, one overhead light,
winter-dark stairs going in,
our enough is enough. My years of it too.

But who gave the body piece by piece
to holy cards, Saint Agatha's
breasts on the plate she held. Her face sweetly
can't look.
Or the Sacred Heart really a heart, the robe
pulled back to a stunned *other*
perfectly bloodless, crowned with thorns
centered upright in the chest.

In fact, it favors the left
and tilts right.
Every childhood is strange. To be
that thoughtless
furious in there—lungs, blue-black arteries
all pulsing a life
to be lived. Be careful, surgeon,

where you cut. So evening,
early spring. Careful,
keys asleep in the hand,
car to steps to door.

Portrait

Of all things, my mother said.

Modigliani. My Aunt Virginia's
preposterous knockoffs, her way with a brush
as they slowly came to.

The trademark long necks. Women always,
each face with its
endlessly vague expression she
multiplied. How many hung on the wall?
Many. And the *why* in me
is a boat
and a hopeless navigation.

I try to imagine what I never saw: my tall aunt
bending herself into their
narrow charm, head to head with one
on her easel, last touches to cheekbone and brow.
But then, she looked like
those women: regal, the sweep of neck, same
blank overseeing-my-kingdom aimed
down and at
until I dissolved.

My aunt, clearly in love.

And if paintings are mirrors and it was
self-love, well, bully for her.
And beyond? *Come deepen me:* part anything
we cherish before getting
lost at sea all by ourselves, bewildered
by those waters, cobalt blue

being best.   Or it's
lapis she chose for eyes
distant, to the ends of the earth
in that house.

Little Wife

at the Oriental Institute, Chicago

They redid King Tut splendid,
once stone-huge as this
yet his wife's feet
tiny, the only thing of her now
low, next to him. A few toes, some of the rest,
a bit of ankle, that's it
in the shade of her husband's looming, massive
looking straight ahead into the future
where we live and can't
eye-to-eye, where to stare at him
is to suffer *warbler neck,* head back and up
à la the high just-leafing-out trees as bright bits
wing their blink
and hide. Little wife,
such small feet, the thought
dwarfs the king
as ache, as what is
ever left of us
and oh, I like her better.

Bolus

Word for all of it sent down there: worst meal,
best meal, most memorable barley and mushrooms,
the lemon's bite that
bites, any old slop made with love or indifference,
savored or rushed, rain pelting
window, kitchen in need of a good scrub, veering
toward toxic, finally the same
same ever-ending
you-know-what. Not a subject
for this pool of thought.
                              You could drown
in thought. A bolus
of thinking into the waves, seabirds with names
you almost knew then pretty much
forgot. *You,* fake bolus for *I,*
a tinker toy, that wheel you dreamt
the baby swallowed,
and there it was in the x-ray afloat like some
crown of His Majesty Who's-It, tiny
pretender to the throne. I mean a mini-
thick-enough disk with holes a kid sticks
a stick into. What a find for a bee,
for the bolus in his gullet
about to be honey. Sometimes it is
                              a sweet thing
and at any rate, I woke.
Why and wherefore and what of it?
Every childhood flash to be treasured mucks up
as bolus, every regret
part bolus that won't go down. And happiness must be
briefly what's left after some particularly stubborn
bit of bolus fields the next round in its descent,
oh lunch tube and past the dark furnace in the middle,

intricate twists of colon, small
then large. Patient, greedy,
both take what they want, dizzy molecules to work
bone and blood, the rest
lost, at last—
                    no, we don't know what.

The Pope under Glass

The pope under glass, the body
of the pope, red embroidered slippers of a pope,
a pope's plush red beanie, the eyes
of the pope closed a minute or two and he's back
in Bergamo, in seminary, still Angelo
the unnumbered, his buddies
happy drunk in the next room and then
they're singing.

Above him it's bad news forever. Such a huge
Saint Jerome framed, afloat on his
deathbed, ravaged as the guy under the bridge
in my town, the one wrapped in three
sleeping bags—standard long straggly hair, gray,
ditto the beard—whose sweet moments
mean it hasn't rained, hasn't snowed, a day, two days.
So the plastic dries out.

In Rome, this churchiest
church imaginable, vast dazzling hive long ago
built of honey and spit. Only it's quiet
up where that very skinny Saint Jerome
keeps dying in swaddling clothes fit
for a baby, where he'd eye with alarm the lion
lower-left corner
if he hadn't once loosed a thorn
from that paw, and if you add wings, it's
Mark, Saint Mark

who wouldn't hurt a leopard, who—vaguely now,
some woodcut?—morphs back
to a man eking out his gospel
with a feather, miscast

in luscious medieval robes. One skull.
Black ink on the table.
Or that was Jerome. Eternity's
not too accurate.

The pilgrims line up with earphones
that leak: muffled e-bits of Italian, smudge
of English, distant pinball of French
and Japanese. They file past
the glass coffin, arrange their faces reverently
to say nothing much, same exact
disappear in it. Pope John is

so white. There are chairs
if you want. I want, I want.
Next to me, a nun at her rosary,
her holy rumble
slow, not yet past a third Glory Be.
We've been here—
how many lifetimes does it take?
Five trillion. A guess.

Tears in Reverse

A tree backlit suddenly
means dawn out there. The black shape

a grayer shape. It takes time
transforming a planet.

Luck is a couple of eyes to see it.
A *couplet* of eyes

to save it for later, wily
invention on paper the big bang could

have flared up to double
a small depth of words, drift,

hold—you go under
in the white space. Truth is

a lake at each eye's pointed corner
called *lake*. A tiny hole, the *puncta,*

in that lake of salt and sorrow, or not
(your rolodex does carry

happiness, as in *weep for,*
less common yet standard).

That pinpoint—tears blink back
into it, into the head

they came from, down
an intricate dark.

That's why you turn away,
why it's so private, why

your nose runs when you cry.
Grief in reverse

might well
be joy. A welling-up

hard in the chest, catch
and catch to throat, that no way

to breathe. Each
and anyway. All of it

from before, into the
years and years.

Turn

So crucial the model in life-drawing class—
we take turns when he oversleeps
and doesn't show. Me, my turn
on the platform, sinking deeper into my sweater and jeans.
I close my eyes to fend off
their eyes. Just so and forever, those
gleaming marble figures at the British Museum,
they look through blanks, time

wearing off color the Greeks
put there and there. What colors? *Dreadful ones,*
the nametag told us briskly, *you know,*
like day-glo yellow. Blue. Green.

Any words that come to me. And the mouth,
a line of ash on their paper.

Thread

at Goya's Self-Portrait with Dr. Arrieta, *the Minneapolis Institute of Arts*

Better to walk toward the painting until
the ghouls get swallowed by dark.
Two faces shine human—Dr. Arrieta, even Goya
who leans against him upright
but collapsed. Arrieta forever offering water
and water, takes Goya's shoulder

to take him where—
no place to go now. Old Goya dazed,
ratcheted up by Arrieta's
relentless doing, his not looking particularly
interested in doing, not heroic or pious, thinking
something else surely.

Behind doctor and patient, those demon heads
afloat in perfect bile—my two steps back,
they're back—are really the ones
keen on the outcome. Or it's simple transport,
a job description: they're
Death. And guess what? Not the famous
single figure who waits but a small
dismal crowd to carry us across.

His painting as *gift*
is the story in the story. Because Goya did
get well. And gratitude is a warmth,
then a weight. Or it can
morph into empathy until self itself
drops out of the portrait. I wonder what Arrieta
thought, where he hung it, how
anyone can stare very long into his own face, who,

who *is* that…. Shrewd of Goya, and kind,
arranging it so the real doctor would
never meet the eye of the painted one whose gaze is
skewed, beyond, as if
grimly-about-to-be-lost sooner or later
passes through him too.

Walk closer. Very close, even that
shimmer of doctor goes out. Blackened weave, canvas
made of thread, unbroken thread
or a small knot
at the heart of it. The shuttle's big loud
isn't loud.

Rom, du bist eine Welt

from the headstone of Hans Barth, buried near Keats in Rome

One vast ceiling in this city—
of course of course, Adam reaching a long way
to touch fingers with a god who
maybe is curious.
Two panels over, Eve takes an apple from
a human hand. We know better.
It never was a garden, how that arm morphs
from the snake of all snakes
a few feet away.

The old story. Threat,
meet dread. The deepest deep sea.
Or outer space with its
light-years flashing through dark.

But never to end
loops and still breaks, color
violent, muddied, murdered in the making.
Paint toxic, a blue scarce-brilliant out of
Khyber and Persia, scaffolding so
look down, day grueling day, the most
twisted position to do
an angel's wing right. Years, the swearing
up there, swirl and swell of rage,
the bad light

huge in the eye
that blinks back an ocean.

A Vision

His long underwear, and that time
carrying his overnight
slop bucket, spare room through kitchen,
flicked sign from our mother, her
cease and desist over eggs or
oatmeal, days some said *grammar* school,
still *arithmetic* at a tablet,
the Virgin Mary eked out to
high plastic on a shelf.
Old, older than prayer, than any
buzzing in the trees, any should or you
shouldn't, his looking not
left or right, fixed
slow, the union suit stained,
stretched, the split back
a backside. *To ghost*
is a verb. The body fits or
it isn't. The Beatles about to be
bigger than Jesus, my brother wise-guying
secret bolts from the blue, me
to my hiding and hidden, head bent
over the last most vapid
good-girl book. Broke off in space
a room, my grandfather in it
zoomed midcentury, born
to the lost real one,
left, little town downstate, silent
ticking house he wound
and oiled with a feather.
Night soil, a name that
looks away, his hand gripping
the metal rim. The worst
is kindness. To see

like it's nothing, our zero to his
gone, going invisible
doomed delicate step and step
by step by now.

My Ears Aren't Right

When bodies floated up out of their graves after the hurricane,
I had no TV to watch.
But too much rain
can translate anything to unspeakable.
First it's awful,
a downpour, my yard out there, the last
worst place for insects that can't
burrow deep, even secret ones
they haven't yet pinned to a lab board, haven't
crowned with little white slips to say so.

No human is ancient enough to grow wings. No human
remembers enough for the long antennae to know
what eternal is, meaning brief, meaning
only this one time. Sleep
isn't death but both are wet and dark and I can see where this
is going and I don't want to. I don't.

Where does it come from—the sound
of the funeral, hymns
they won't sing now, too complicated, too minor-key slippery
and steely, old lace with such holes in it,
what smokes up to smart or choke
out of the chained censer, an arm raised
to swing forward, drop back, the walking
nowhere with it, battered
metal click of the thing dreamt
sixth century, black shine of those troubles,
Latin no one understands.

Anymore, my ears aren't right.
It's the weeping
held barely by a floodwall.

At the Keats House, Rome

How long is this posthumous life of mine to last?
JOHN KEATS, THE MONTH BEFORE HIS DEATH, 1821

Even to think, any of it—
Just draw, I thought.
And note color in his room for later because
what a mess I'd make in there.
So I wrote words, the wall
not quite robin's egg, the floor's old dark
a maroon. I sketched
with pencil: window, those tiles underfoot,
scribbles framed for paintings,
a big boat bed of shiny mahogany, my lines
barely, as long as they would
mean in the end, a guide for Rome once,
halfway across the planet.
                         And weeks would slip
before an hour or two,
my watercolors, at home: to work
the way poems get made, like memory knots and unties,
most immediate verb—*is is is*—trading up
any past life to eternal present, trick of light as if
there is no shade. Keats did,
then he didn't get better.
His room is part-lie, his TB wrongly
certain the plague where Vatican law aimed
its trumpets. The real bed? They burned it.
And bedclothes, the heavy curtains, wallpaper ripped
ceiling to floor. God forbid
what he breathed out stay. Letters he couldn't
bear to open, brave
keeping those, probably illegal, think
more unpretty, *buried with him,*
a shovel, ten minutes

of falling dirt. Not *starless, moonless.*
Funny, we put people in the ground
when they're done with us.
                              Whoever looks
sees the Spanish Steps from
that window, their rise and ruin crooked as an old,
vast accordion where the thrill is
it widens, a giddy slow motion, exhausting.
And the wheeze—
though I heard only shouts, laughter, traffic sounds.
The fountain there too, a modest affair
of the other Bernini, the sculptor's
unfamous father, marking the most distant spot
the Tiber flooded, its shape
a small boat that foundered, broken thing of stone,
and the spray—*anyway, anyway*—
delicate, continual.
                          Noise can sometimes
be music. Or a fragment,
a sentence. Or month blackening month
can reverse, luminous as x-ray. The hand
holds a pencil to find—at last! for a moment,
no moment. That's what it is
to make drawings. The loose ones give way
as though happy
and sad meet best in some
blurry afterlife where neither will ever know
more than the other. Keats. His death mask floats
in that kind of plexiglass box screwed to the wall,
his once-eyes closed, his once-face
a face, eerie greenish white plaster.
                              I erased and drew again.

Looks like he's dreaming,

doesn't it? Who was that in the room,
her of course I'd get
what she said, that she wasn't alone where
her English jarred but in all of Rome—*Roma!* —
this sacred place for it.
Dream, the usual code for mystery,
for figuring any last bit: past into present,
life, death, great poems,
no poems worth the reading or why anyone
would write them. Or she was simply
nice, being nice, stranger to stranger, because that
language in the street
how Keats must have heard it—part racket,
part high-held note, and mostly
a veil. My distracted
                              no answer at all
was unkind. And not
even true. See, the window had to be right,
the ceiling brought down by pencil
to paper, same same
flower, inlay after inlay carved
to a madness up there.
                              He's sort of
beautiful, she said, tentative
as translation.

Practice Saying

So practice saying: my name was—
what exactly. And why did I live?
Then those words the poet, the quiet one, puts
into a mouth. Spit them out.

Not all of us get to be ghosts.
A few still need a good
googling, or the Ouija board sitting level on knees
to ask stupid questions. No matter: we'll
all telepath into the ether.

Will we be another species then, strange and endearing
as a cat that talks incessantly? I had one
one time, a little much
though such sweetness, her insistence, her
wanting to tell me at every turn.

What a puzzle death becomes, rainy afternoons
to put who we were
back together. Certain poems begin
with a pine tree in the middle, or a bird yet to be found
in any Peterson guide. Good. That's

great. Call it *in* life or
of life, before
the before and after
rolls into one giant look-down-upon-
the-well-of-all-being.

Here. You know
where that is? Little dot on the horizon
that isn't a flower,
isn't a man walking home.

Human Atlas

Because the body really
is Mars, is Earth or Venus or the saddest downsized
Pluto. Can be booked, bound, mapped then.
Or *rendered* like something off the bone, fat just under
the animal skin, to lard,
cheaper, quicker than butter, like stillness
belies restlessness, like every yes
was or will be never, no,

                           none of that.

Such a book keeps
the skeleton so untroubled. To narrow in, to say
femur, rib—a suspension, a splendor—
to stare like that
stops time. Or slick pages and pages given over
to slow the blood, remake muscle, to unsecret
that most mysterious *lymph,* its arsenal
of glands under the arm, at groin, at neck, awful
ghost lightning in it. Inscrutable.

                           Complete: because
the whole body ends, remember?
But each ending
goes on and on. Complete: because some
minor genius with a pencil, with ink, with drastic color
makes that arm you've known for years
raw, inside out, near wanton run of red vessel and nerve,
once a sin to look, weirdly now,
what should be hidden. Oh, it's *garish*

                           equals *austere.*
Compute. Does not compute. Tell me.
Then tell me who that
me is, or the
you understood, the any of us, our precious
everything we ever, layer upon
bright layer.

How Hair Is

How personal
hair is: wayward expanse on the chest, the teenager

thrilled by hair under his arm at last,
wiry squiggle at the groin.
Or my great-aunt Nell deranged near the end,
a nightgown
thrashing the sheets, her red hair not faded but flaming
that spot.

How personal when they
turn the male cadaver back to front, second week
of dissection lab, mostly gray the tiny ringlets where ribs
make their switchbacks for now.

The heart in there to the left, quiet,
lungs either side maybe
once flushed with forced air from the ambulance flashing
street after street, cars pulled over abrupt
as if impatience

were homage. Not anyone,
this one, this one who breathed, who unbuttoned a shirt
to the broad, specific
tangle of it, rarely looking down. Not really a field gone to scrub,
to low thicket. Night

hovers night. The smallest rise
in that leaf mould.

Like unto Like

Someone told me no big deal.
Go ahead, translate *Tod*
into *toad*. Death in German—
why not such a creature "at my shoulder."
So that's the way: you shrug,
you give it a shot. Out of ceaseless mucky
muck and weeds, death at collar,
at ear, shrunk
spring-locked to the page.

Like unto like. Thus any medieval herbal,
book of remedy and remedy.
Or later *The Signature of All Things,* 1622,
where a leaf still turns up
healing, the heart-shaped digitalis to
unstrange a rhythm raving,
sweet blood and slow blood through
the muscled dark.

I'm a sucker for charms. All at once she
slipped or she flowered or she
deepened or she darkened. Evening,
the saint's heart, 1308,
nuns find a tiny crucifix, their knife after vespers
to stare her open. Prayer
a sting, a stutter
until years, the whole business stained
minor key. Think what that
sounds like in the middle of the plague.

It's not exactly. We never
want the same.
Now and then I wake at night.

Only shadow equals
empty enough, equals sideways when
an arm, a leg....

The moon, how it
cannot know. Except I saw it fall—
room and window and across the bed
brief, as in
to earth there.

Knowledge

The glassy eight ball floating up cheap prophecy
yes   no   try later,
a white triangle, the black letters.
I did try. Spring, or it was
summer, me in my shorts on the sidewalk,
making my pact. There's time, this lasting forever.
Never childhood to a child.

We lose names of things. Then the things
they named. Oh Babylonians,
who slaughtered the sheep so its smoke turned prayer.
Praise, or a bribe.
What they really wanted—the liver,
organ of all-knowing,
in a temple, out of the sun.

One mark—you,
by yourself, always. Two marks: you earn
your enemy. Three: good news! he's
dust. Opposition is all. So is endurance.
That blue-gray lesion? The river will burn black.

More to read right in that flesh: desire,
motive, the usual damage to
greater damage. *Don't*— a very very dark in the left lobe.
Famine turns up
white as a rash, a speckling. The zones—for real—
Station and *Palace Gate* and *Path*.
Or my favorite, *Yoke and Increase.* You have to be
part optimist, like: fate equals bad,
destiny, not so bad.

In Anatomy, in lab, I did see a student
lift out a human liver.
Careful. Her gloved hands rose from the mess of his body.
Not love, that pause: *to be*
amazed by. They kept reading
a faint stain
to follow down. Fate behind the pillars
where something fell.
He probably thought future like we all think
in our blur of intentions—a grand place,
an okay place.

The Souls of the Dead

My grandmother, her oddly accurate
euphemism, *turning up to the doctor.* She meant
caught in stirrups on the examining table,
a doctor warming
and wincing his speculum to eye
the most interior goods.

It's just that in lab, they're tying open the legs now,
the cadavers supine. They're pulling them
to the end of each table, knees roped sideways. *I am so not
doing OB/gyne*—the most brooding
first-year med student is shaking his head.
Like I can't believe I'm writing this
word by word until *I can't believe I'm writing about this*
stares back at me from the page, mildly
unthinkable. Narfia, the anatomy TA: *We try to be
so respectful....*

It jumps gender. It's *equal opportunity.*
The male students put off
dissecting the penis. *Just another thing left to women,*
one of the women blurts, *like WE
want to?* My grandmother, her other roundabouts:
a tablespoon of bourbon in the pantry each
afternoon late, her pick-me-up.
As for my sponge bath, I was to wash down as far
as possible. *Don't forget possible,*
she'd stage-whisper outside the bathroom door.

At the museum, a small "threadcross" behind glass,
back dimmest
whenever-it-was to capture bad spirits against the slow
rise of a mantra

said just the right way. A trap woven at the roof
or the entry of anything, to keep safe,
to ensnare.

We bent to my favorite, the 99-year-old. I told her
this won't last. Sure I did, sure.
In the great pyramids, the Harpy tombs had Sirens, female-headed
birds, really jars in secret, holding
the souls of the dead who peered from all four corners.

Read the Gesture

It's perhaps not terribly hard.
He walked into a room and could not look at us, etc.
Not just grief.

At times the body speaks only of itself
with such forceful
modesty: I limp therefore I am something-
bad-going-on-in-there.
                                  There, via torn ligament or
long bones, short bones,
the ends meet wrong. Whatever joint
not *quite-ing,* the surgical press to verb up
past the anatomists, their staid lust for words
that elevate and hide the real thing.
                                       He walked into a room then
(by way of his *vastus medialis*),
he could not look at us (see *levator,* most definitely
superioris). Latinates mangled, piled up big
as the Sphinx, body of a lion, head of any human who might
stare across the desert to hope a simple line
of raging wet nearby, how as a kid
I pictured the Nile. About to flood such lush silt
is a great story,
                 a gesture, a generosity.

Then the child disappears
to go on, to think the rest of it—the sweat,
the worry, the look of a bent back
at a distance
                 beginning early,
a blister rubbed
raw from the hoe.

Even night is a gesture, sleep
a cog in its wheel of stars. Lie down.
At some point you lie down.

Mind and Body

Whether blood alone does the knitting
over the wound, I don't know. Whether the chitchat
of the surgical nurses—a daughter's quote unquote *boyfriend,*
or mother-in-law as genus and species, or which
the better napkin at Thanksgiving, cloth or paper—all
presses into the brain
of the anesthetized woman to *do* something,
I don't know. Doesn't any blather assume
a next day and a day after that? She-of-the-shiny-table
hooked up to a zillion clear tubes
under the force-fed light would have feigned a most
cheerful interest, even a point of view—cloth, absolutely.
Whether *this* turns *that* in the worst
circumstance, I don't know. It's hard to stand still
in rain, in fog. There are pieces of war
only the dead can bear, horses in old photographs
bloated and leveled, trees
cut to the nub. That's the first shock
before what might be
human bodies in the foreground. And whether
woods get *autumnal* for a reason,
leaf on leaf flaring red-gold just to fall down, dream
in spite of the real afternoon, I have no idea.
Whether childhood matters, I don't know that.
Whether broken bones there,
the split knees and lip, confessions
unconfessed, trips alone to the basement's dank underworld
quiet in its way as the ticking clock made
the room upstairs, if that
matters at all to strengthen bones now, to attack the baddest
bad blood cells in the universe,
I'll never know. Whether the brain has
hobbies other than notions

of a possible afterlife, angel or
no angel, loved ones lined up radiant after the train wreck
of getting there, for the long wait to see us again—
who the hell knows. Whether one *can*
get better, better than what dark
goes on in vessel, in chamber, the blind ride
down the nerve—I'd have to take
night, flood it with day
and more day. Whether
whether even counts as an option
in genuine truth-telling—shouldn't that be
a thunderbolt? Minus
the *should*. For that matter, minus
thunder too. It's
the bolt: to be *beside*
oneself. To know what happened,
what has to.
Oh yeah, says the body ever after,
quite out of body.

Hands

A whole roomful of hands—
drawing hands! Then I know I'm thinking too much.
My teacher said *keep looking* when I figured
done, the broken-off
conté crayon in my fingers.

Early spring, wired urgent with spring
means the catbird
never lets up, his small chaos falling
again, again to the telltale whiny note,
the *meow* of no cat
I ever heard. In reflexology, you press hard
between third finger and the little one
to dull such ringing in the ear.

The hand in cadaver lab—the first fully human thing
we did, I thought. No hands alike, raging
small vessels run through them—you'd never
believe how many ribbons. The arm
kept springing up, no
not to volunteer. We tied it down with ordinary rope
you'd get at the hardware store, and even then—

The catbird is gray and dark gray but you can't
see him, not with the trees
leafed out. That hurry in a throat, no sound
like another he repeats
sideways, down,
inside out.

A whole room of hands drawing hands!
I still love that. Look away then. You should
look anywhere else

in that other room, hands with a knife to dissect
the hand, no fat there to speak of, busy
traffic of nerve and vein and tendon and trust me,
it stops.

II

Cadaver, Speak

The body—before they opened me—the darkest dark

must live in there. Where color is wasted.
Because I hear them look:
bright green of gallbladder, shocked yellow fat, acreage
flat out under skin. To think I brought this
on myself.

No blood in the lab. No longer
my blood, paste flaking
brown to the touch, the heart packed with it.
They do that too.
                    Let it pass, my husband said, for years.

But you know what? It's more, it's how
there is no sleep. It's how words
come apart in a dream.
And then you're awake.

Pale nerve, bluest black veins. Muscle gone gray
but still pink in places,
fanned out or narrowed, tendon-strict,
white elastic to knob of femur,
humerus. How on earth

to tell this. That they see things hardly
anyone.... Things buried, doing
for a lifetime. Sunken
                    bonehouse—what body, my slow mineral ruin.

Darkness at the start. It sticks,
it bothers me: why any color at all?

Room of echo and stink. The silence we contain, we
cadavers now, water
that dumb and overflowing.

> *Blessed those—*

too young to be stricken. They're kids,
in their twenties. They stare, they keep probing. To idle
amazement, to trespass like that.

Is it brave? What's *brave?* You know
then you unknow. My God, how they walk into this place
to begin with—all the ways in the smart ones, this

must burn
right through them:

> *Pure Spirit, stupid me good, just to stand here.*

1

Unique. But each the same.
They strip for this drape out of
jeans and those T-shirts,
ready, this fit-for-sacrifice.
Blue scrubs given first: pants
cleaver-cut quick, sewn wide,
a shirt over the head by way
of its V, the belt
a length of cord pulled up and held.
They tie it
like my daughters tied shoes,
looking down and so serious.
First a loop, only to circle
and pass that through slow
as if to practice
practice
how time is made. I remember
minute circles minute, seconds
slip off
and tighten.

White lab coat torn at the pocket.
White lab coat, a button gone missing.
White lab coat, white lab coat repeat repeat,
a refrain, months, weeks of
white lab coat bleached over and over to
human, faint stain at the cuff.

2

Silver faucets to the wall. And light from no window.

Four tables broad enough, slick-shine enough for us
to be turned, to come apart one muscle, one intricate webwork at a time.

That whirl, a machine that tries and tries and cannot—no, the air isn't sweet.

A plastic tub with its label   *spinal cords.*
Two three four empty ones already marked   *brains.*
Drawers with their   *hammer   chisel*
                            rope   handsaw
                            Virchow skull breaker—

Fluorescent little ice cubes up there, bright basement room.

Boxes and boxes of purple rubber gloves
cool, insistent as shadow.

3

And once upon our time: we were two men,
two women. Heart or lungs did us in
old—me the most, my ninety-nine years. Here in the lab
they're told that. So do I
win something? Me, third in line
on these tables. Only, before they cut, they imagine
we imagined them
imagining us as we made this offering
for all humankind, one of those
hero movies, our signing the paper,
desk of black wood and chrome until
who *was* that?—stranger or niece or grandson—call
from the hospital. Or kitchen, so much closer,
more urgent,
terrible, my daughter's half sandwich
left to a plate.

Post-yes: we drifted there, spring
and all summer
sunk in glycerin, ethyl alcohol, whichever
evil chemical. I forget.
It read like a recipe for Boilo at Christmas, but that's
sugary and thick, each steamy cup,
cinnamon in it. Cloves. The new year.

He must have been a farmer, some
med student said. Why? Because he's
a big guy?—the second of us
laid out here, huge.
The quiet one, not really
in the class, who puts a caption on every
little thing called him *the cadaver pinup,* the
cadaver *hunk,* so sure she was funny.
In fact they're in awe of his hands—even she is—

the massive chest, the whole works, his
smallest nerve, muscle,
almost an Oldenburg, she said, perfect vast
exaggeration, to be set in caps.

Like you know what a farmer looks like.
Someone else said that.

4

People say a lot of things. And think
three times that many. Nothing like this place
ever crossed my mind.
                              But my sister, the artist
in the family. She had
a book—Da Vinci's big pages—
and I'd lift it down to show you if I could,
Italian on one side, English
on the other, not a mirror
you step through. But *to make* like that
                              took the ten bodies

he claimed. Or thirty—liar—
he finally owned up to,
dissected and drew. I get it now. A knife
sees things. Then ink from an oak gall,
and a favorite red chalk, and his
universal conditions of man.

Was one of them *Mirth?*
                              The first one, thank God.

Was one of them *Weeping?*
                              He put that second. As in *tears come from the heart,*
                              not the head.

The third, was it *Contention? With its acts of killing—*
                                             He meant *flight   fear*
                                             ferocity   boldness   murder....

And *Labour,* was last? I seem
to remember the *pulling   thrusting   carrying   stopping*
via little levers in the body, how they
work beyond reason, little weather within,

rage and loft of sinew taken to pieces
page after page.

        The one hundred and twenty books composed by me—

Leonardo, so stuck on yourself!—

            will give verdict
            yes or no.

5

Long underground passage to get here
early morning, all fall—so I picture them walking.

These are the catacombs, the quiet one lulled herself

and scared herself—
telling the whole lab, probably everyone in creation—
at least three weeks in.

Oh angel of the familiar, of the *too* familiar,

erasing all wonder—

Then it's *on time.* Or *late.*
The elevator door opens to a hallway, to get through.

6

What to hate most: this mummy way they've
wrapped our heads, thick wet towels
close, in orbit. Or the distant shock of it

I half love. The pretense that
they've blinded us. So they can work, of course,
without our staring back. *Work—*
first taking down and out what's left of us,
gristle by gristle, siphon to sprocket, their silver probes
in those empty bits, all new words—my *fossa—*
is it *fossi?*—where the edge
of bony things once fit. Only they see
what's pooled there.

But it galls me—that even my dismemberment's
so predictable: my back where they little-windowed out
my spinal cord, then the slapstick flip right-side-up to shoulder, arm,
hand, on to plot my middle kingdom: liver, spleen,
down to *possible,* my mother might have said,
shooting me that look.

Nearly a century on Earth gives a person
permission to be crabby
but not an idiot. When people write, I like
sentences that turn sudden,
unexpected. But that
didn't happen to me. I gave away
then wore out my ending.

When my family talks, the usual blah blah goes on:
Generous. And such a good long run!
But I never ran,
not ever.

7

Who hasn't walked by those museum cases—
heads bandaged up, the entire body in there.
It keeps coming back, that word
mummy. And somewhere—
maybe a TV special—how they soaked strips of cloth
in resin first, layer on layer
of winding down and around, packed with mud
from the Nile, all to give a body
shape. I still covet
little facts. I collected them, like things
hidden in those layers, for later—
bracelets, charms. Such a glorious later.
What would I put
in my coil? A locket from my father who got it
from his mother. A daughter's baby tooth.
My husband's old driver's license, his looking not
into the camera but astonished,
straight up, like he's seen something.
The mud so wet and lush and cool in the heat
of that place, so *back then.* I've read this: those wrappings
announced "a transfigured being."
The *appearance* of it, the book said.
Well, any radiance is good, isn't it? To be
someone else for a minute, for
a while. Or so I tell
the self I had. Then this: the ancient head and limbs
got wrapped first. Thus our heads
in these towels, see? All four of us. And our hands
and feet in these soaked tube socks.

8

I did go to college. Nothing fancy,
one of those normal schools. I was proud
of that, smart enough, up
from the one-room schoolhouse, the old story—
a girl off the farm,

                sort of a rarity. It wasn't exactly.

I liked words. I liked
to read—*Aesop's Fables,* Housman. Frost by heart,
the story ones especially. I loved metaphor
though nothing's really like anything else. I loved Trollope
and Dickens. Not Jane Austen—

                        she lied. Things don't

mainly end best though there's a chance
with *better.* I taught school some. Didn't care for that, no.
You have to be bossy. You have to be
certain about stars and how words rhyme, how
dollars cartwheel up and over and again

                          to make Johnny rich.

I just kept reading.
So what's this fellow got to say all the time? my husband said,
holding my Frost to his ear, shaking it
like a box a voice might fall out of. *You should write
your secrets too!*

                No secrets, I said. But I

thought about things alone
and eyed my girls like a scientist as they grew—
if too much sleep would make them
stupid, if their quarrels were tied to weather, a beautiful day
and its boredom until

                the spark and flash

of one simple meanness
bloomed sharp between them, for a change.
Change means: what happens
in secret. I happened, they happened, she he it happens,
a day, then a next day.

           Oh to write, the way people do.

9

Is it merely what happened, happens again on the page?
That so-be-it whoosh, the usual
suspect as speaker, the fortunate one lost then darkened in the cloud and
        the privilege?
                        No no no no! Voices, take over, a poet says
                        from the start. Cadaver, speak.

        Sure I want them bright red red red! Why the hell not?

That's the first cadaver, the other old woman, what
she must have said just before.
Before. Imagine.

                Week Three: Upper Limb. The soaked tube sock pulled
                like an evening glove from her hand.

And can't we pretend this the opera—
wouldn't she of such fingernails say that?
She'd call it *Knife & Shriek*.

        Ha! Let's pop their little eyes out!

                You bet those fingers flashed. Bare breath sucking in, then
                they laughed—delight—two bodies down from me.

10

The things they leave willy-nilly at the end
of these tables, the morning half gone.

The breast they cut from me
to worry the milk glands, those

tiny wires one daughter
turned from, the other

took with her beautiful greed.
My husband's greed was sweet

and fierce. He hid it in the dark.
That, I miss.

11

One of them here—the bookish one, who loves stories—
says it's uncivilized, says no, he won't
touch the electric saw, black cord dangling
from the ceiling, a saw so smart
                              so smart
it stops quick and cold
when a living hand fumbles in the way.
How can it know

their knuckles from my ribs,
their silence from mine,
their standing-over from my
lying-here, grim costar
in all this undone and undoing?

That's not a question
but a story. Not a complaint but
a chant. Not a boat
but water beneath and ongoing,
whitecaps small and they jack-rabbit
vast, such a bright day
on the lake, and sky, and mountains,
snow on those mountains for my

nevertheless, my no-pain-at-all.
The tiny saw
is the one that screams
when it hits bone that kept my lungs
keeping on, and pinned there,
restless years. The smoke of me
rancid, snaking up lazy
the light in this place.

12

Of course, the four of us—we died, didn't we?
Gone months before anything
happens on these tables. We had names
someone might
still say in passing, might think
before bed.

Is that solace?

Ninety-nine years old: I'm small.
One of them touches my shoulder and her hand
stays there.
Then I am smaller.

Smaller than.... My grandmother
who curled like a fish
every afternoon nap, too wry and loved
for one life. I watched
from the doorway, followed her spine's
knotted half circle
in that blue cotton dress.

Identify, appreciate, move on: this
teacher's good mantra.

                    (And if I can't move on? Or she can't? Or
                    he can't? Or any of us. Or all of us.....

Have we appreciated enough? says the med student Josh
to the med student Ajit, staring down
the start of my vagus nerve's flat white
endlessness. From the brainstem south, its journey
famous and fabulous radars out
to ear and lung and heart, all various
mad viscera in my lower distance.

Vagus. Longest run
in the body. I understand these things now. I am
these things. Never poor little nerve.
From the Latin, *to wander.* Thus *vagabond.*
And there's *vagrant.* Same root
of old when gods
walked the earth in disguise, ordinary,
vague enough.

13

You know me. You saw me in the shops, on the street, in the dentist's office.
The dentist! Thank God I'll never do that again.

I was that old one who made you crazy, picking up every apple
and putting it down. I blocked the display on watches,
their little faces silver or gold, because
I couldn't decide.

Next to me—not the giant—it's the last
of us on his back, too. He opens
like a box cut down the middle, flaps made
to pack him back up when
the day's work stops. They roped him hard, every
which way to turn the hand so they could *do* the hand,
and almost broke something. And now
when the whole getup gives or slips or whatever
rope does, his arm
drops to any old arm in the world thrown off
in sleep, off the edge
of that shiny table. Like it's a bed. Like he
just turned over because his wife
poked him, he was snoring softly but way
too loud for her. She had a dream
to get back to.

Such a human gesture! Who wouldn't
look twice at that arm, blinding half second.
You would too.
I just mean: the dead know the ways of the living.

14

Love. It isn't what
I want. I'm past that here. Past fear,
past hunger, thirst. Past dreams

bad or good, past
past. Except things move
and blur like you see from a car

no one drives now. Clearly I'm
still curious. A message curls
in some bottle flung up on shore.

Was there ever such a bottle?
Real cause and effect,
a favorite of mine. Not math.

Just the neat miracle of
the obvious next thing. The quiet one,
she pressed my aorta—

the *crack*
of hard plastic. She sprang off
like I hit her.

15

You'd never guess the way
one of them put his hands around my heart, hoisting it
high as a baby.
          Hardly rocket science, as people say, to say that.

Still they take turns with it, pretty much oohing and aahing
though no,
no bright beastly cry lets loose.
My lungs too.
         They're almost

velvety, another boy says. Why, how like a pet—
is that it?—the kind you love to touch, sent to its corner
to sleep in a rhythm, both such good doggies.
But lungs don't match
in shape or size, each a fully
separate fiefdom. I learned that here.
A curious pleasure as these doctors-to-be
press every side soft.
         My breath's still there, a breathing.

The last poor racket I made probably, dreadful
middle of the night.

Toward the end, my arthritis not
too bad, I wanted to draw because
my sister did, you know. And maybe that
would bring her back. I wanted a self-portrait
so gorgeous the world would startle
and stop. Right. But I took a class.
And the boy next to me in studio, at the local college,
who knew so little English, taking a break
from his own mirror and easel, walking around,
he pointed at mine when I turned, his
Munch!—amazed, throwing both hands to cradle
then narrow his face, awful O-gape of the screamer.
That painting, so famous it's funny,
on T-shirts now, lunch boxes, who knows
where else. My sister—
she would have laughed until she
nearly choked at what the boy blurted out. Not that
long ago. I could have been one of the models
we older students liked best, not
the theater majors who pose like they pose, those
beauties still immortal, knowing everything wonderful
about to happen. I'd be in the other tribe of bodies
worn hard, to sag and line, to ache
and faded scar and a fully
limited insight. Dear boy,
smiling in the middle
of his broken English, so certain he was praising.
I looked back at my *Munch*
for the first time: the open mouth,
endless black
and white prophecy.

17

The air in this lab, the thing they
talk talk talk of. I already said—
not great. And it sticks
to their scrubs and their hair.

Me, my rot at the heart of it.

Not my fault. I soaked months
to clean up. And here, every late afternoon
before I'm plastic-wrapped for the night, they spray
alcohol and water and *fabric softener*
all over this
body of rags strewn out on the table, my
flag of no allegiance stripped
to its zillion bad colors between worlds.
I'm so many pieces!
But this new trick of the elements—passing
into ether. Once stars and planets
famously made from it.

So—I'm at this party, right? says the med student
Claire, *and   oh   my   God,
I smell cadaver on me!*

I'm like that now: secret,
loyal as a whiff.

18

Today's postcard is: two young women float over me,
knives and probes down, into—

a cloud of furious busyness.

Because they must *know* things, and to know is to
find them first.

But it breaks deep: a shot, a *report*. Their urgent
oh no.

Another cloud to darken me. Stop.

And neither says, until one: *It's okay. We'll be doctors. We'll know
how to fix it.*

19

As a girl I...

Isn't that a way never to begin because
who was that girl?
This dissecting table and how I fascinate
under these lights and their questions—
an excuse to live forever.
But you can't begin
what is over.

As a girl I thought
war was over.
Over, its newspapers yellowing
on the porch. My father
rolled them to a fuse
and lit the furnace.
The sound of airplanes still
made us look up.

As a girl I knew the dead
meant clothes my mother gave away.
My aunt came and put them
in the good car. My brother's shoes in the mix,
brown and black, a uniform too,
gumboots for the farm.
I got his dog.

Then later came and mainly went.
Let's face it: most of it
is later, grown up and so smart,
changing every bit of it back there.

The thing is—well, so many things.
But nothing's original.

To find the colon, those gleaming twists
and turns, they cut and cut and bend back the muscles
past the ribs—not *at*
the ribs where heart, lung, whatever else live such a sheltered life—no, lower,
barely the abdomen, a cut
clear through to the most glamorous chain mail.

But you see, it's soft. And spreads out
like it's woven: *the greater omentum,* glistening gold bits of fat, tangled
threads by the million—
                    The very first bubble wrap! one med student says,
his hands at my pelvis
where it slowly flaps free, unpinned to anything. His lifting it—
to what gods?—is sacred, *a veil,* to draw
that aside.

And the quiet one, her mind so empty
sometimes even I can read it.
I know she's thinking—
                    So this is how
they got their big idea.
The Catholics' tabernacle, the Jews and their Holy of Holies....

I could have told her I'd bring back
the beginning of time.

My father loved to *reckon.* Reckon this,
reckon that. By which he meant
thinking. And my uncles, always *recollecting*—
about livestock or the war, about weather.
That's a mulling *back,* to pull it out of pure dark
until it stands still against
all elsewise.

Here they memorize me until my parts
could be anyone's—that's the point, isn't it?—
though not the hands. They're mine completely,
my oddball double-jointed thumb prized
and passed down from my mother.

Like when they finally unwrap
our wrapped heads in this horrid fluorescence,
we are perfectly *not*
one another. *Yes,* the quiet one says in her
deliberate italics: *so beautiful, like*
those Renaissance drawings, exactly who they are….

So, would Leonardo do me up this
exactly— excuse me—that I'm left
the most toothless, dumb-witted of hags?
His charcoal crooks my head on its little stalk
back—no, not a flower. But some
cobalt in his kit that day.
A thin watery blue still floods each eye
in real time.

Such beauties we are now—yeah, sure.
And until the quiet one figures everyone's
sick of her saying it, she's
stunned. Stunned!

Nothing like my own staring
straight up—

22

My husband said
I had a way with words. Usually that meant
I disagreed with him, something
about the house or trouble
with the girls. What words I had—
I admit I could throw
so fast, they'd
break things. But I could
whisper too.

In this lab, such a flood of ponderous
thousand-pound Latinates! So the homegrown ones
leap out dear
as a joke: the hand's *Anatomical Snuff Box* where
thumb snaps back to make
the most charming
sunken spot you put the vile stuff.
Or empty space inside, back
near the back, for what?—*Pouch of Douglas, Pouch of Morrison,*
like two houseguests driving off
forgot them. And the skull's small craters as if someone
entered with a candle to claim
Meckel's Cave, passing on
his bloodless lineage. Little *junior.* O little
named-after-me.
               The anatomists sweeten their lists.

I know, I know, I'm important here—
like my intestines, crucial, making everything

wet and small enough to matter.

Day one, the teacher said: *These are your*
first patients. Take good care of them.

Trust me, they do. And wouldn't my mother

have relished such attention? *My social life*
is going to the doctor, she loved to tell

even strangers at the end. My own

case in point: that young man, Ajit, who
rubs my shaved head now and then

for something more than luck.

I know they're all pirates in this expanse,
treasure to be seized and claimed

to the tiniest ear machinery—

my incus and malleus and stapes.
What a roaring to let in—most

miniature drum I beat senseless in life,

wave on wave, to hear anything.
Ajit leans close—to me, to my ocean.

24

In Italy—I saw this the one time we traveled—mirrors on the walls
more black than silver, worn out from centuries of faces
looking into them. I tried getting closer. Something
moonlike reared up in that glass, bitten off
parts of a moon.
Dark dust streamed like clouds.

The teacher tells the quiet one: enjoy these heads while you can,
before we skin them.

He holds back the worst.

Because first is how that saw
jolts up again, and they bowl-haircut my skull and lift my brain
like a cake from a box.

Are they thrilled or what? And what's left of me in there—
the times I finally, or wanted so hard but could not
or would not, or didn't know for a lifetime
I had. *Cool,* someone says, *if only we could wire this baby up*
to a computer and play the ninety-nine years
of her movie.

The worst?
No mirror could tell you.

25

My brain soaks in a bucket. You give and it's given.

So why and to which high cheap seat is
night and day,
                    is *only you beneath the moon*—

the tiniest piano
down there or somewhere I wake to over and over,
like I wake to....
                    Or my husband's bath, his hands hit

water I keep hearing. First to bed, I almost slept.
How it sounds at night, the warmest
next room of him to me.

26

What we rattled off by heart in school: *Oh what a piece of work*
is man, how like an angel, how noble in reason, etc etc.
Hamlet's right. It's all wrong.

And not because I lie here like this.
The body's wired plain enough, nerves off the spine, off that
old knob-and-tube of vertebrae. And I admire
how heads wobble on their *atlas,* C1. First stop
on the cranial highway, named
for that poor soul stuck forever, world
too heavy, heaved up behind him.

No. Because nerves madden, they overreach.
It's the hip's L5 haywiring down to fire up
the toes. What a ridiculous run
of body miles!
Then the tireless rerouting, over years, city built
on city, next and next and so messy. A neighbor nerve
replaces what's broken. Or a restless one
hitchhikes a second pathway.
Some disk in the spine turns rock to shatter its link to arm
or leg. More amazing: that these
jerry-built circuits spark at all.

We start simple, the teacher tells these kids.
One cardiac tube in the womb.
One gut tube.

Look at me. There's more, just wait. We grow strange
                    we grow strange
                    we grow strange
                    we grow strange—

So they do, they skin the faces. *Our* faces.
Really a mask then, was it? For years.
But to change that,
                    to make us *beautiful* again,
the quiet one puts
a metaphor's distance between:
no, she says to anyone, *we're just*
shaving him. Or *it's just they're negatives of themselves now,*
everything reversed for a moment....
Meaning where
                    light should be, bone
gone out, or—
how can I know? She's arty, that one.
Delusional. But the first of us, the finger-polish lady,
morphs to what they'd show off
in a gallery or some glossy book, only half of her skinned—
little *half* mouth, *half* nose,
one eye and cheek down to its x-ray.
The other side they forgot, got lazy or had
reason, still full-fleshed pink—
                              was I ever that pink? She is
beautiful. One artery at night,
how it throbbed straight from the heart so close to my ear
to keep me awake.
                    They pulled that apart.
Not a head,
a skull. Not an eye, an orbit.
                              But the truth about negatives,
ghost behind any photograph—
fixer, stop-bath once pooled two little trays, a bluish
half-light in there. Could be
it comes again
watery, unspeakable
                    and I'm back to myself.

28

An odd place to consider
courtesy. But such rituals of kindness take over.
Love, whatever

that might have been, first ran
as a ho-hum set of

nothing much. *That's fine, no problem*—
when clearly it was. The way one of them,

I'm sorry to me
when her knife flashes wrong. *I'm sorry,*
so sweetly.

29

The worst
is ancient, a chant
or a charm—
              They took off our heads.
If I had to write
that most balanced, simple sentence,
I'd need the steely posture
I never had.

What hard work. It takes time.
Not for nothing they
invented the guillotine.
One of them here, Geeta of the lovely black hair,
hacked away
so dogged and never glanced up.
                      Look, even the tough
worldly one who figured out
in seconds what
nail polish that was—*rose madder red*—she
stepped back. Then I knew it
way worse than the rank yogurt mess
they found in one lung.

Certain minutes
pass, go stark, you count
forward and slow and
you breathe.
            Oh yes. My head
jiggled loose—
broke off—my stump of a neck. Most
medieval unbearable fury—
                   lean in
for the drop.
But no one threw it.

30

I forgot the bit about the rubber band, the longish kind,
each one of us got a different color.
Mine was blue. And for a while when they finished
with our heads each day, they set our skull-bowls back
on each brainless void, our
flaps of scalp *secured* with that rubber band whose ink
ran a blurry orbit. And our crew cuts seemed
filled out a little.
        Is it true? the quiet one asked the teacher,

what Whitman says? That hair
grows after death? His answer: *No.*
But that put a poet
in the room. Then another. *John Keats dissected, he*
trained as a doctor, can't you tell? the bookish one chimed in
to quote, to prove it:
        Here, where men sit and hear each other groan;
        Where palsy shakes a few, sad, last grey hairs,
        Where youth grows pale, and spectre-thin, and dies;
        Where but to think is to be full of sorrow....

He trailed off. No, both,
both of them. I swear to you—
        what kept singing?

+ + +

And now, here: the-never-will-be
was. Which is to say,
the rest could be said by anyone, I suppose.
Past tense for *not yet*
is *oh, that.* For *today*—
last week, last month, yet another Wednesday shot.
There's spring
because of winter. Before that,
fall backed into summer where rain
linked sun like some split-second lurch in the car.
Past tense of *window*
is *close it, such weather.* Past tense of *pain*
is *sleep through the night.* Before *cut here,*
sew up, cauterize (you smell something burning?)
is *rot,* is *wound,* is *cold* then *colder.*
Before war
is war. Before peace,
more war. I waited, I worried
was my bloodless lot. I remember
the stopped heart,
and before, *nothing you'd notice.*
That *nothing* on and on, huge
and years, weighs
about nothing, like
a whistle's sweet because
it's distant.
So many meant well, telling me *God*—
God this, *God* that—like
they know. Well, I never knew.
There's the body, there *was*
a body: what they found in me
in that lab
is proof. Past tense of *me,* by the way,
is *she,* a woman who lived—where

was that street?—who worked
on the farm, at school, in the dirt, at a desk,
in the shade; who read, who forgot
what she read; who drove home
after so many deaths too fast, too slow,
the last corner, the house we once
and once I wouldn't
get out of the car. *She*
who played not one instrument, even badly.
Past tense of past drifts
into ruin or myth or
did-it-happen-at-all. I won't even ask. I dreamt
same as you do. I did.

Acknowledgments

Warm thanks to many for their response to some of these poems or their progression *as book,* which helped me see more clearly: always—and first— David Dunlap and Will Dunlap; then Joy Manesiotis, Brigit Kelly, and Ellen Voigt; and also Charles Baxter, who introduced me to Goya's painting *Self-Portrait with Dr. Arrieta.* Many thanks as well to my good-hearted coreaders who first brought the title sequence before a live audience, on four separate occasions: my fellow residents at Bellagio, then the medical students and the poets enrolled in the graduate writing programs at both Purdue University and the University of Edinburgh, and, later, theater director Christopher Beach and students at the University of Redlands.

I'm grateful to Purdue University, whose Faculty Fellowship for Study in a Second Discipline granted me the privilege of a semester in a life-drawing class and the gross human anatomy course of Indiana University's School of Medicine, the so-called cadaver lab where I was allowed to be "the quiet one." Gratitude also to Gordon Coppoc, head of that IU division on Purdue's campus, and certainly to my two thoughtful teachers: anatomist James Walker and artist Grace Benedict. Thanks to the Rockefeller Foundation for the Bellagio residency that aided and abetted the first draft of the title sequence, to the American Academy in Rome for research time, and to the Anderson Center (Red Wing, Minnesota), which gave me a place to write other poems in the first half of this collection. Thanks as well to Purdue University's Center of Artistic Endeavors for the release time, and to Emma Black at the Surgeons' Hall surgical museum in Edinburgh for access to that fine collection. Most especially I'm grateful to the Fulbright Commission, to the University of Edinburgh, Scotland, and its Institute for Advanced Studies in the Humanities (and its fine director, the late Susan Manning), and, of course, to the College of Humanities and Social Sciences on that campus and its distinguished program in English literature. The generous welcome I received in the UK enabled me to complete these poems. So this book came together.

I am indebted to the editors of the following journals for first publishing poems from this collection: the Academy of American Poets website ("Poem-a-Day"), *The American Poetry Review, Crazyhorse, The Edinburgh Review, FIELD, The Hudson Review, London Review of Books, The*

Massachusetts Review, Michigan Quarterly Review, Narrative, The New Yorker, Poetry, Poetry Review (UK), *TriQuarterly*. In particular, I'm grateful to Stephen Corey of *The Georgia Review*, who saved back an unthinkable thirty-one pages for the sequence, allowing my cadaver to speak all she wanted for the first time in print. And to the Magazine Association of the Southeast's GAMMA Awards committee, which gave a gold medal to that long poem. Thanks as well to editors Eleanor Wilner and Maurice Manning for reprinting five poems from the sequence in *The Rag-Picker's Guide to Poetry: Poems, Poets, Process* (University of Michigan Press, 2013), and to editor Elizabeth Hurren for running one of those poems in *Wellcome History*, the journal of the Wellcome Trust, the visionary support agency for medical humanities in the UK.

Finally, regarding the image on the cover of this book, I need to thank Susan Ryerson and Richard Rubenstein, two of my compatriots at Bellagio, for the story of Saints Felix and Regula and their servant Exuperantius, all of whom, it is said, walked uphill carrying their heads after their martyrdom in the third century, looking for just the right spot to bury them.

About the Author

MARIANNE BORUCH is the author of seven previous poetry collections, most recently *The Book of Hours* (Copper Canyon), *Grace, Fallen from* (Wesleyan), and *Poems: New and Selected* (Oberlin). Her other work includes two books of essays, *Poetry's Old Air* (Michigan) and *In the Blue Pharmacy* (Trinity), and a memoir, *The Glimpse Traveler* (Indiana), about hitchhiking the lost world of the 1970s. She was born in Chicago, survived its parochial schools, and graduated from the University of Illinois and, later, the University of Massachusetts at Amherst.

Among her awards and honors are Pushcart prizes and inclusion in the *Best American Poetry* series. She has received fellowships from the Guggenheim Foundation and the NEA, a Fulbright Professorship to the University of Edinburgh, and residencies at the Rockefeller Foundation's Bellagio Center, the MacDowell Colony, the Anderson Center (Red Wing, Minnesota), and Isle Royale, the most isolated national park in the United States. *The Book of Hours* received the Kingsley Tufts Poetry Award in 2013.

Places she has taught or still teaches: Tunghai University in Taiwan, the University of Maine at Farmington, and, since 1987, Purdue University, where she developed and directed the MFA program. For many years she has been on the faculty semiregularly at the low-residency Program for Writers at Warren Wilson College and occasionally at summer conferences, including Bread Loaf, Bear River, and RopeWalk. She and her husband live in West Lafayette, Indiana, where they raised their son.

Lannan Literary Selections

For two decades Lannan Foundation has supported the publication and distribution of exceptional literary works. Copper Canyon Press gratefully acknowledges their support.

LANNAN LITERARY SELECTIONS 2014

Mark Bibbins, *They Don't Kill You Because They're Hungry, They Kill You Because They're Full*

Malachi Black, *Storm Toward Morning*

Marianne Boruch, *Cadaver, Speak*

Jericho Brown, *The New Testament*

Olena Kalytiak Davis, *The Poem She Didn't Write and Other Poems*

RECENT LANNAN LITERARY SELECTIONS FROM COPPER CANYON PRESS

James Arthur, *Charms Against Lightning*

Natalie Diaz, *When My Brother Was an Aztec*

Matthew Dickman and Michael Dickman, *50 American Plays*

Michael Dickman, *Flies*

Kerry James Evans, *Bangalore*

Tung-Hui Hu, *Greenhouses, Lighthouses*

Laura Kasischke, *Space, in Chains*

Deborah Landau, *The Last Usable Hour*

Sarah Lindsay, *Debt to the Bone-Eating Snotflower*

Michael McGriff, *Home Burial*

Valzhyna Mort, *Collected Body*

Lisa Olstein, *Little Stranger*

Roger Reeves, *King Me*

Ed Skoog, *Rough Day*

John Taggart, *Is Music: Selected Poems*

Jean Valentine, *Break the Glass*

Dean Young, *Fall Higher*

For a complete list of Lannan Literary Selections from Copper Canyon Press, please visit Partners on our website: www.coppercanyonpress.org

Poetry is vital to language and living. Since 1972, Copper Canyon Press has published extraordinary poetry from around the world to engage the imaginations and intellects of readers, writers, booksellers, librarians, teachers, students, and donors.

WE ARE GRATEFUL FOR THE MAJOR SUPPORT PROVIDED BY:

THE PAUL G. ALLEN
FAMILY FOUNDATION

WHERE LESS IS MORE

golden
lasso

Lannan

THE MAURER FAMILY
FOUNDATION

NATIONAL
ENDOWMENT
FOR THE ARTS

WASHINGTON STATE
ARTS COMMISSION

Anonymous
John Branch
Diana and Jay Broze
Beroz Ferrell & The Point, LLC
Janet and Les Cox
Mimi Gardner Gates
Gull Industries, Inc.
on behalf of William and Ruth True
Mark Hamilton and Suzie Rapp
Carolyn and Robert Hedin
Steven Myron Holl
Lakeside Industries, Inc.
on behalf of Jeanne Marie Lee
Maureen Lee and Mark Busto
Brice Marden
H. Stewart Parker
Penny and Jerry Peabody
John Phillips and Anne O'Donnell
Joseph C. Roberts
Cynthia Lovelace Sears and Frank Buxton
The Seattle Foundation
Dan Waggoner
Charles and Barbara Wright
The dedicated interns and faithful
volunteers of Copper Canyon Press

To learn more about underwriting Copper Canyon Press titles,
please call 360-385-4925 ext. 103

The Chinese character for poetry is made up of two parts: "word" and "temple." It also serves as pressmark for Copper Canyon Press.

This book is set in Minion, designed for digital composition by Robert Slimbach in 1989. Minion is a neohumanist face, a contemporary typeface retaining elements of the pen-drawn letterforms developed during the Renaissance. Display type set in Adobe Jenson, also by Robert Slimbach. Book design and composition by VJB/Scribe.